"I Lov A Turkey Butt Samwich"

Finding a Farm Life After Hollywood

A COLLECTIONS OF READERS' FAVORITES
FROM HER "I'M JUST SAYING" COLUMN

BY PAM STONE

Stone's Throw Publishing

stonesthrowpublishing@gmail.com

ISBN: 1475132638
ISBN-13: 9781475132632

For the long-suffering and much appreciated Paul as well as all the 'woofums, hoofums, and pussums' of the farm

Paul McCallister

SPRING

SUMMER

AUTUMN

WINTER

SPRING

"I Love Me A Turkey Butt Samwich"

"Let me ask you a question," said one of the gals who works at my local feed store, leaning conspiratorially toward me, over the counter. "Have you ever eaten turkey butt?"

Always interested in pursuing original banter, I replied, "You mean on purpose?"

"Yes," she said, looking sideways at her co-worker, Keith, who was, at that moment, engaged in trying to hone his rodeo skills by roping a salt block.

"Nooooo," I replied, having created an image that wasn't sitting well with the Lance "Captain" crackers I'd just ingested. "Can't say that I have."

"Well, he has," she said, jerking her thumb. "Isn't that the grossest thing you've ever heard?"

Keith, having missed his third attempt with the salt block, turned to champion the cause of poultry posterior.

"It's good!" he defended. "In a sandwich. With bream."

"Bream?" I spluttered. "Like, bream, the fish?" This was truly appalling.

"Yep," he replied. "I love me a bream and turkey butt samwich."

That took a couple of seconds from which to recover.

"I could see eating that if you were in the Donner party and your choice was turkey butt and bream or your brother," I said, "but there's no need to eat that way. I mean, you can get something at McDonald's for a dollar. Although the turkey butt and bream is probably healthier."

"It's goooood," he maintained.

And then I had to know how on earth he came up with that combination in the first place. I mean, I grasp the concept, if not the desire, for a fried bologna sandwich or a cupful of "livers and gizzards!" now being advertised at the local Spinx station.

But who sat down with the tail end of a turkey and,

pondering what could trump the taste, elected bream?

"Ah, I used to live in Florida and did a lot of fishing, and there was always a group of guys that would come by and want any bream that I caught, because I used to throw it back. But they're the ones that turned me on to it and, really, it's good!"

Naturally, one had to ask, "Well, what's turkey butt taste like?"

"Different. Kinda crispy. It's pretty dark."

You don't say.

But this is what I love about small-town living. While the rest of the world is blogging about the rise of the tea party or fighting traffic or moaning over the Christmas music already being played in shopping malls, one side trip to the feed store led me to some information I could actually use.

One day.

If I'm desperately starving.

Or want to weasel out of hosting future Thanksgiving dinners.

The Ride Of The Polkyries

Knowing all too well that guests were arriving in a matter of days and realizing I had yet to replace the stained dining room rug or do something about the sofa, one arm completely shredded by the cats, I had allowed myself to run out of time and was now aware of a creeping sense of panic to get everything done. This instant.

Feeling the self-inflicted pressure procrastinators often experience, I gunned my dually up the Saluda Grade to find the rug of my dreams (on clearance, no less!) at World of Carpets in Hendersonville and, after delivering it triumphantly back home, realized I had but half an hour to pick up my sofa from the upholsterers in Mill Spring. With a shudder I looked up at heavy black clouds, hanging low on the horizon and figured if I drove like Dale Jr. I might just make it to the shop, get the sofa loaded and skedaddle back home before the heavens opened on my new, carefully chosen, sage green brushed-cotton trophy.

There's a prayer to St Jude that I often see published in local newspapers that promises if said for 9 consecutive days, ones prayer will be answered. I didn't have the luxury of 9 days but rationalized if I blurted it 81 times, I might just beat the rain, so as I slung the truck along Highway 9 all the terriers heard above the din of the engine was, "St Jude, help of the hopeless, pray for us....St Jude, worker of miracles, pray for us…"

With a spray of gravel, I pulled up in front of the shop, threw down my money, muscled the sofa into the bed of the truck and then flew back down Highway 9 towards home. A scattering of tiny drops hit the windshield. I threw the truck into 5th gear and, at the same moment, caught sight in the rear-view mirror of three green cushions sailing through the air, reminding me that I had specifically requested that the old cushions, originally sewn to the back of the sofa be unattached so that cleaning would be easier.

The terriers eyes bulged at the torrent of language flooding through the cab as I stood on the brakes, shoved the engine into reverse and before the Tahoe behind me had the chance to turn the cushions into road kill, leapt into the street like a mad woman, gathering them into my arms, waving traffic to go around and then chasing the truck which had begun rolling with two shrieking Jack Russells at the wheel as the emergency brake hadn't been engaged. Jumping breathlessly back into the truck, it became evident that St Jude was suddenly called away to find a lost wallet or someone's wedding band as it began to rain in earnest.

The whole point of living in the country, in my view, is that everyone knows everyone else and folks are willing to help their neighbors. There is also a theory that one could be savaged by a Chow-Pit-bull mix should one arrive, unannounced, on a stranger's property. Realizing the only protection I had was an empty Big Gulp cup that I could hurl at anything that might meet me with unbridled aggression, I jerked into the driveway of a modest brick ranch, tires squealing, to pull beneath their carport and wait out the rain.

Within a couple of minutes a screen door cracked open and a grey haired woman asked if she could help me. Oh, I just needed to get my sofa out of the rain if you don't mind, was my reply which seemed to satisfy her, although she mentioned that green wasn't her favorite color and it would show dog hair. A few moments later she reappeared to offer me a glass of tea which I declined and, after that, she wondered if I wouldn't mind dropping off a stack of newspapers at the recycle center if I happened to be passing that way. I was and before long, with a great heap of paper separating the dogs and skies that began to lighten, we began our trek home.

I couldn't help but wonder if I would have been able to take such advantage of a complete stranger if I still lived in the city. In Los Angeles, I probably wouldn't have actually seen the owner of the home, but, rather, would have been explaining myself while handcuffed in the back of a police cruiser, or, depending on the neighborhood, would have been ignored with the exception of a spray of graffiti across my vehicle. But somewhere in Polk county is a woman who took the whole episode in stride as she has with everything else she's probably seen living out in the country: rabid dogs, coon hunting at 2 a.m. and bored youths clobbering her mailbox. At any rate, I thank her kindly.

And, ma'am, you're right: it does show the hair.

The Adventures Of Booger Cat

Any sense of drama that I might have must come from my mother. She tends to be rather theatrical at times which can range from, "I can't find my keys!" to "My stove won't turn off and it's going to burn down the house!" The latter, of course, is deserved of a jump from 0 to 60 on the octave range, the other, surely less so but it does add a flair to normal mundane conversations. Her impeccable, English accent is simply icing.

I speak daily to my mother on the phone, usually by 8 a.m., just to check in. Usually, the conversation goes something like this:

"How are you?"

"Fine! Duke Power finally had that limb in the front yard

removed that was hanging over the power line."

"That's good."

"And IGA has some lovely plums for sale,"

"Really?"

"I simply cannot believe what that Dick Cheney said on television last night!"

So there is always a tremendous amount of information to be gleaned from each call.

Things seem to happen to my mother. This may secretly please her because it results in more dramatic stories to tell. I enjoy it because it's more original material that I get to blab about on the radio. The latest adventure involves a neighborhood thug: a recently abandoned, calico Tom, that my mother has christened, "The Booger Cat."

Booger Cat belonged to an elderly woman who has moved from Mom's neighborhood and simply left him behind. Perhaps with good reason, although, as an animal lover, it grieved me to hear his fate. Mom disliked him intensely as he would sneak up on her own pride and joy, a tabby named Chloe, inflate himself in front of her on the other side of the living room window, spitting and hissing. Chloe, in return, would screech and attack the glass and then flee from the room and hide under the bed.

"That wicked, wicked cat!" Mom exclaimed the following morning at 8 a.m.

"Poor thing!" I said. "He's been dumped. Maybe you could feed him."

"I'm not going to feed that brute! Chloe is still under the bed and scratched me when I tried to comfort her!"

Within a week, she was feeding that brute. It began by leaving a chipped cereal bowl of whatever kibble was on sale at the IGA. It escalated to her crouching by the bowl, last week, as he was eating, and extending a gentle hand to stroke which he promptly attempted to ingest.

"I've been savaged by Booger Cat!" was the opening gambit the following morning at 8 a.m.

"Let's have Katy drive over and have a look at you." I said, referring to my sister, a nurse.

"I already called AARP! They have a 24 hour nurse on duty and she said to get to the hospital straight away and get a tetanus shot!"

"Let me drive you then."

"I already went last night! And now they want Booger Cat."

"He's got to get a tetanus shot?"

"No! They want to put a cage out to catch him and take him away."

"But they'll kill him!" I cried, matching her octave. We were probably making nearby garage doors open an close at this point.

The plan, I later learned, was to quarantine and watch him for a few days, but I didn't buy that. I just knew they were going to put Booger Cat down. The drama increased over the next several days as each morning, a new, unwilling, captive was seen to be glaring out of the cage that had been erected on Mom's front porch.

"There's a raccoon in the cage!" I was informed at 8 a.m. on the dot.

"Can you let him out?"

No! He's messed in it and has walked off wearing it and he's now in the middle of the street, turned upside down! The entire cage is crushed and you should smell the trail he's left! It's all over the porch, up the sidewalk..."

"Mom! You can't leave him upside down in the middle of the street. Go pick up the cage!"

"I'm not touching that wretch! He's probably riddled with rabies!"

The raccoon was later released and I don't know where the

cage is. But I do know when Paul and I dropped Mom home after Paul's birthday dinner last Saturday, I caught the glimmer of nocturnal eyes, dazzled by the headlights as we turned the car towards home. It was Booger Cat, in all his majesty, sitting on a rock wall opposite my mother's house, washing his face.

"You'd better scat, cat!" I said, leaning out the window. "You don't know how lucky you are!"

He paused, his damp paw held just below his mouth, and regarded me as one regards a rather limited, uninspiring, menu.

Some cats are just like that.

Valentine's Hay

'Soooooo," cooed one of my dear, recently "involved" friends, "what did you get for Valentine's Day?"

From experience, I know that relationship neophytes are never really interested in an answer. Their polite query is for the sole purpose of giving a breathless report of what their "wonderful, new, man" gave them on the Big Day.

"You start," I replied.

"Well, I just couldn't believe it. First, three dozen red roses. Then a copy of 'Leaves of Grass,' and he booked a room for the whole weekend at The Grove Park Inn — we're going to have a spa, dinner, the works!"

Awww. Don't you find it sweet when people are in the blush of new love? When everything is heady and dreamy; when they haven't heard for the 27th time that his mother wasn't demonstratively affectionate, resulting in a difficulty with intimacy for you? Before the object of love is discovered to have bodily functions? It's nice. A little obnoxious for the rest of us, but nice for them. I don't begrudge them a bit.

I stand with a lot of people who have been in a relationship for so long that we vaguely recall (or was this a movie we recently saw?) feeling giddy when seeing a flashing message on the answering machine, or being amazed that someone is really interested in our life story — at least the first time the tale is told.

Like many of you, I don't need a Hallmark holiday to manipulate my fella into bringing home a box of chocolates like a cat at the front stoop with a dead mouse.

It's the same expression, really: "This is for you. You do want it, don't you?" But he does. He's a good man. And he's a good man every day. I'll take that hands-down over a weekend at The Grove Park Inn.

I will say, however, that this time I was armed and ready to reply after my friend finished her litany of gooey items.

"That's nice," I said. "Paul filled up the truck for me, and then we drove to Clemson after he got off work to pick up a load of timothy hay that was only $8 a bale and so, even with the price of gas, we still saved about $150 compared to buying it at the feed store."

My friend could only work her mouth wordlessly.

Take that, Cupid.

Lionel The Mini-Mule

It's a quite common sight: a stray kitten is tenderly brought home in the arms of a round-eyed child, proclaiming, "But it'll die if we don't keep it!"

Or...

a thin, wormy, female mixed-breed, freshly torn from a litter of puppies is kicked out of a car on a quiet road. This I expect: we live in the country. We've already taken in the above, described, most dearest of terriers. What I was completely unprepared for, however, was Paul coming back to the barn one freezing morning not too long ago.

Normally, when Paul returns quickly after leaving for the nursery it's because he's forgotten his wallet. Or laptop. Or office keys. Or pants.

This day was different. He drove his Honda right up to the barn where I was nearly finished mucking out.

"Do you have an extra halter I can borrow?" he asked.

Now, c'mon, that's a loaded question.

"Someone's dumped a horse up at the nursery." he went on to explain.

"A horse? Someone dumped a horse?" I said, in disbelief. "How big? What size halter?"

Paul leveled his hand around mid-chest. An experienced, equestrian eye would figure that to be about 15.2 hands. I grabbed a "Cob" sized halter and jumped in the car with him to appraise the latest foundling. When we arrived at the nursery, one of Paul's employees was holding by the mane, a thin, shaggy, chestnut mini-mule, all of about ten hands in height. He could have worn the halter as a truss. I looked at Paul. "Your sense of perception seems to be off."

"Well," he replied. "I saw him from a distance."

This from the man who built a linen wardrobe for me that we, literally, could not get it into the house. He also purchased two rocking chairs for our front deck that are exact replicas of that giant chair on the hill on the way to Pumpkintown. I find him to be a latent admirer of Paul Bunyon.

Anyway, that's how it began. The mystery of Lionel (named after the curmudgeon character in the Brit sit-com, "As Time Goes By") became a bit clearer when it was learned that he had been removed from one field for chasing calving cows and broke out of his confinement at another place. We heard through the grapevine that the owner was quite relieved that we had taken him in. We tended to his overgrown hooves, gave him his shots, wormed him and received a kick in the thigh for our efforts. The vet said he was "somewhere in his thirties."

Paul is enamored with him. He led Lionel home from the nursery with a newly purchased, jaunty red halter and lead. A winter, foal-sized, blanket secured the animal from the biting winds.

When he arrived home, he was introduced to his new room mate, my twenty-six year old draft horse, Moose, and immediately lay down in a fresh bed of shavings and fell into a deep sleep. In the morning, Paul was up before dawn, bringing his new pet an armful of hay and breaking the ice in the water trough. He was head-butted for his trouble.

A man and a mini-mule. It's a beautiful thing.

Playing Doctor

There was quite the emergency last Friday at the farm.

While answering e-mail in the office, Paul, mightily impressed by this year's contenders on "Top Chef," could be heard in the kitchen dicing an onion on the chopping board.

The steady tap of Wusthof on wood was suddenly aborted and replaced with Paul yelling,

"I need a Band-Aid!"

Sighing, I rose from my chair to hear, "I need two Band-Aids!"

By the time I strode up the hallway, Paul's plea was amended by, "I've cut off the tip of my finger!"

Probably because I've had horses my entire life and horses have a magical way of impaling themselves on anything unnoticed to the human eye in both stall or field, I have dealt with many an injury that would rival a war wound. So a bloody finger was no big deal. In fact, it was slightly refreshing.

Paul stood, looking slightly pale, over the sink, blood pouring from the top of his middle finger, the tip adhered by a thin strip of tissue.

"What do you think?" he asked in alarm, trying to staunch the bleeding with a paper towel. "It's bad, isn't it?"

"It is very bad," I agreed. "Who's going to cook dinner?"

A couple of minutes later, with a sandwich bag filled with ice enveloping his hand, I drove him to the emergency room, where we were to spend the bulk of our Friday evening. Other people might have found this depressing. I, however, was blissfully in my element.

You must understand that I am a card-carrying "cyberchondriac." There is nothing I like better than to get on the Internet and research symptoms and unravel the process of elimination until I find a particular diagnosis that makes sense. This, naturally, led to me believing I had every disease known to man and Paul had to forcibly remove me from WebMD.com when, numb with fear, I whispered hoarsely that I was quite sure I was in the latter stages of testicular cancer.

However, now alongside my man and waiting for the doctor to come in, I was happily eavesdropping upon symptoms being discussed from behind various drawn curtains.

"Have you been dizzy?" I heard a nurse question the anonymous patient behind us.

"Yes, and so tired," was the reply.

"Frequent urination?"

"All the time."

"It's diabetes!" I nearly yelped, but was thumped to silence by Paul.

The patient to the side of us, I suspected, was having an anxiety attack and I was dying to ask the doctor the results of her EKG, but again, discretion persisted.

When it was Paul's turn, I, of course, insisted on a tetanus shot and gave the harried doctor my opinion that stitches, probably at least five, were required.

This was met by a world-weary look and the doctor silently began to clean, numb, then stitch, the wound.

After bandaging the finger, Paul, trying to inject a touch of levity into the situation, was given the opportunity to use a line he'd always dreamed of saying:

"Doctor, will I be able to play the piano after this?"

The doctor, rising and pushing up his glasses to rub his tired eyes, said, "Of course."

"Great!" said Paul. "I've never been able to play it before!"

This was met with another silent stare before the doctor turned on his heel and left the cubical.

"Tough crowd," Paul remarked.

"He looked a little pale," I mused. "Probably getting no sleep and not eating well. I suspect anemia."

OK, for the last time. It's Pam.
Not Sharon!

For the second time this past week I've had the embarrassment of being mistaken for a huge, Hollywood, celebrity.

Sharon Stone.

Now, how cringe-worthy is that? One is a glittering, sexy, gorgeous woman and the other is, well, me: dirty hair squashed beneath a baseball cap, dried horse sweat caked on the inside of my riding boots and built pretty similar to a Pez dispenser.

It's been happening for more than a decade and the only theory that I can come up with is, while I enjoyed minor celebrity from appearing for seven seasons on a successful sitcom, I was nowhere near being a household name but people had a vague notion that 'Stone' was involved and, because they certainly couldn't remember my first name, the immediate flash that came to their brain was the most famous: Sharon.

I remember keenly this happening for the umpteenth time while performing in Las Vegas. During the day I enjoyed walking the strip and doing some shopping. In a crowded mall, a man followed me from The Cheesecake Factory all the way to Ann Taylor, continually barking, "Sharon! Hey, Sharon!" Annoyed and wilting from embarrassment, I refused to acknowledge him until I stopped for coffee and, turning on my heel, hissed, "I'm not Sharon."

"Sure you are!" he insisted. "Can I get your autograph? I used to watch 'Coach' all the time."

Well, what are you going to do? Dutifully, I scrawled "Best wishes, Sharon Stone" across a napkin and wondered how he would frown, perplexed, when all his friends raved over his close encounter with such an enormous star and undoubtedly ask, "So, is she as gorgeous as she is in the movies?"

Leaving television and Hollywood 10 years ago and transitioning into radio I thought, surely, these sort of confrontations were well behind me.

But only this past week, as I signed a receipt confirming installation of satellite television at my mother's house, the representative from the company, having said hardly a word during the two hours he labored to get a clear signal, chirped, "Wait till the guys see that I've got Sharon Stone's signature."

Not looking up, I muttered, "Well, you haven't got Sharon Stone's signature. I think she's a little too busy to be in Tryon, right now."

And if that's not bad enough, a mere two days later, obliged to put in a personal appearance with Ramona Holloway and Sharon Decker, my co-hosts from a radio show we broadcast on Sundays, I was approached by Ramona, smiling mischievously.

"Have you seen this?" she asked, tucking a flier into my hand. This was the flier that Lowes Foods, the grocery chain who has sponsored our show for two years, had mailed to thousands of residents in Matthews, to advertise the grand opening of the store in whose parking lot we now stood.

"Grand Opening!" the flier proclaimed in splashy, bold, print. "Meet Radio Hosts, Ramona Holloway, Pam Decker and Sharon Stone!"

"Oh, dear God," I winced.

"Should be a great turn out!" she chirped.

My mortification faded by late afternoon, aided by the good nature and laughs of those who strode over to shake hands and chat.

And, I suppose, like anything else, it could certainly be worse.

No one's ever called me "Oliver."

Name That Business!

When you live in a small town, it's tremendously exciting when a new shop opens. My favorite bit is the dizzy anticipation and the jump-starting of the rumor mill:

"Did you hear what's gonna open next to the Dollar Store? A Waffle House!"

"Now, that's not what I heard. I heard it was going to be a Hardee's."

(This is an actual conversation in which I was involved, by the way. I don't have cable.)

"Well, the fella that did the grading said it was either going to be a Waffle House or a Subway."

"The guy that I talked to who poured the slab said it was going to be a Hardee's."

"Yeah, but if you look at the way it sits back and how the parking area is being graded, it's just like a Waffle House."

Paul and I were like tots with our noses pressed against the window, waiting for Santa, each time we drove past the area in question. We were dying for it to be a Waffle House.

There is nothing in the world better than a brand-spanking-new Waffle House before the walls become stained with nicotine and there's so much grease on the menus that a fly has to attempt a landing like a nervous pilot on a storm-tossed aircraft carrier. Honest- I once saw a fly skid across a menu and crash into the salt shaker. It was just like roller derby.

So imagine our chagrin when what actually opened was another row of storage units. For Pete's sake, how many storage units do we need in the Carolinas?

Most people just keep all their stuff on their front porch anyway. If they're particularly self-disciplined, it makes it to the yard and every now and then, it actually sits by the road, where they know perfectly well it will never be picked up by anyone.

And some of it's pretty entertaining. I've seen goats roosting on the top of a rusted-out El Camino and feed corn beginning to sprout from the seat of an abandoned recliner.

Once, on the way to Lake Lure, I saw a toddler just a'wailing on an over-turned stove and transmission in his front yard with a plastic baseball bat.

Whether he was releasing tension or responding to an innate sense of percussion, I'll never know. What I do know is that had all these items been parked and stowed away in another innocuous row of storage units, we would be missing an awful lot of entertainment.

Which, frankly, from what I've seen, is better than anything on cable anyways …

The Jury's Out...To Lunch!

One of the interesting aspects of small town living is being called in for Jury Duty. Not an appointment anyone truly looks forward to, but one we all generally obey, sooner or later, like a sullen teenager finally picking up his room.

Coming from first, Atlanta, and secondly, Los Angeles, a city of well over 14 million, it was no surprise that everyone in the prospective jury pool was a complete stranger. Being a melting pot, there was a vast array of faces: Asian, African, Latino, you name it- all grim with missing work for potential cases that wouldn't be nearly as riveting as O.J.'s.

However, should you be summoned locally, you will find that, A: you recognize most of the prospective jurors

("Well, hey, Donnie, how's your Momma's hip?") and B: you probably recognize the defendant.

This happened, oh, let's say in February. I have to really be careful here. I don't know why~ you can stumble coming out of the Post Office at 10 a.m. and it will be on "The Tryon Evening News" (aka gossip mill) by 2 p.m., so I'm probably very late in the telling of this story... Anyway, let's say the case being tried was an attempted 'assault with a deadly weapon' case. And let's say that the plaintiff claimed the defendant threw a pit-bull at him and then clubbed him across the head with a tire iron. It wasn't nearly that imaginative, but not only do I not want to embarrass those involved, I realize that, sometime in the future, they could very well be in a jury deciding MY fate, so it's better not to tick anyone off.

The humor began when the attorneys present began, one by one, to interview each potential juror.

"Sir, do you know or have you ever met the defendant?"

"Yes, sir. I hired him to finish my basement last winter."

"I see. Do you think that, having employed him at one time, you could be unbiased towards him?"

"Yes, sir, I do. But he's such a nice fella, I just can't believe he'd a done such a thing!"

"Excuuuused."

A second, elderly, gentleman was asked to come forward and state his name. After frowning in response to several questions, he finally cupped his ear and shook his head.

"Sir, did you understand any of the questions I have asked?"

"Well, it all sounds the same to me like when I was on that other jury last week."

"I'm sorry?"

"I can't make out a thing you're sayin'"

"I wish you had informed us of this, before."

"Well, nobody ever asked me if I could hear!"

"Excuuuused."

The funny thing is, as you sit there and watch what you regard to be clearly inferior people chosen instead of yourself, you forget that you came grudgingly to Jury Duty in the first place. Suddenly, you're the spotty-faced sixth grader who's the last to be chosen for basketball. You begin comparing yourself to the others, thinking, "You have got to be kidding me. He's got whiskey on his breath and missing a thumb!" or, "Not that Holy Roller..."

There is a lesson to be learned, here. If you are new to The area and you think it's possible you might be breaking the law in near future, start baking muffins NOW.

Pass them out to everyone you meet. This way, while they might not quite be what you consider to be your peers, they'll certainly remember you:

"I just can't believe she'd do such a thing. Have you had those pumpkin ones she makes?"

Trumped

Because I chose to drop out of college in my third year and move to Los Angeles in order to investigate the possibility of making a living as a stand-up comic, I've always thought, if nothing else, I've lived a rather adventurous life. Performing gave me an opportunity to visit nearly every state in the Union as well as throughout Canada and Europe. And because most of my friends know me as "Horse Pam" and as horses are all I generally want to talk about, they haven't really heard of this other, shadowy, life I've led.

There are wonderful stories to haul from memory to bore potential grandchildren, had I decided to spawn, so perhaps when I'm 85, I'll simply regale the stuffed bodies of my beloved terriers, Bonnie and Rosie, propped up against the back of the dining room chairs at Thanksgiving, with these true-life tales. They'll look at me blankly, which I'll interpret to mean barely concealed fascination. My one-way conversational nuggets will begin something like this:

"Once upon a time, I had a pit bull named Max that nearly pulled down Jay Leno's pants."

"I'll never forget doing a show from the back of a flatbed truck on a beach in Spain in front of 2,500 sailors."

"You'll never believe this, but one night in London, I literally, on the street, bumped into the actor Christopher Lloyd and the American ambassador to England. An hour later, the three of us were eating strawberries and sipping champagne in Christopher's suite at the Dorchester till 3 a.m.!"

Along with these name-dropping indulgences are also tales of hot-air ballooning in San Diego, flying with eyes screwed shut in a glider above the Bavarian Alps and regaining consciousness in a dew-soaked vineyard somewhere in northern Italy. No, I shall not expand further. It's like an acquittal means nothing to you people.

The point of all these illustrations? Simply to provide a sprinkling of samples, gentle reader, so that you might agree, "Well, this will be nice to think of when she's in a nursing home.

Well, consider me trumped. On all levels.

My English cousin, Hunter, has just returned to his West Sussex cottage after a week's visit here at the farm. He's an interesting fellow who has led a varied and interesting life. Like me, he is childless with adventures tucked away bubbling to be shared. His mother, my late aunt, worked for Orson Welles for more than 30 years and that, in itself, is pretty amazing. The travel required by her spilled over into Hunter's life and gave him ample opportunities to live wondrous experiences. As a boy, he was sent to the same boarding school that was attended by Prince Charles. As a young man, he came of age in swinging London around 1964. Now, I ask you, what is cooler than that? However, not having spent any real time with Hunter for more than a dozen years, there was much about him that I didn't know. I didn't know that he was a model railroad enthusiast. I didn't realize he had once been a surveyor. And I certainly didn't know the best story of all. The story that reduced all my adventures to a crumbling, dried arrangement.

"Did I ever tell you," he began, as I steered onto Highway 9 toward Lake Lure, "that I introduced the 'twist' to Romania?"

I merely gaped.

"Yes, I was part of a youth delegation allowed into this then-Eastern Bloc country, and the kids our age had never heard any rock 'n' roll.

43

"I brought in a Chubby Checker LP, began to show them all how to do the dance and they went wild! Evidently, it spread like wildfire."

The lush countryside pouring along each side of the car turned as dull as 2-day-old iced tea.

It's as if I've never lived at all …

SUMMER

Warshers and Dolls

The phone rang at 7:15 in the morning, the day before the moving sale.

"Do you have a warsher?"

"I'm sorry ... I think you might have the wrong — "

The voice on the other end cut me off smartly, reading me back my own number.

"Yes, that's my number, but —"

"A warsher. Are you selling one?"

Finally, the penny dropped. "You mean at the sale?"

"Yes, ma'am," came my reply. "I need a warsher and a dryer. You got one?"

"Nooo, I'm afraid not, but there's two other garage sales on the same street, and they might have one."

"All right then, I thank you," said my caller, who had clearly taken the "No Early Birds!" statement in the ad I had placed to refer only to a physical presence at my mother's house and not what hour or day he might telephone.

Just as I was hanging up, I heard his weather-beaten voice crackle again through the line.

"Do ya have guitars?"

"Uh, no, sorry. No musical instruments."

"Ukuleles?"

"Nope. No ukuleles."

"I'd love me a ukulele."

Now, at this point, I had a decision to make. Either I was being taken in by my best friend from Los Angeles, a fellow comic, who periodically checked in to shoot the breeze and was known to begin our chinwags with ridiculous accents which I generally fell for, or I simply had a talkative fellow on the other line who might be a bit lonely.

Having been duped mercilessly in the past, I decided it must be my friend, Cary, and gave him a rather large dose of his own medicine. Exaggerating my accent, I countered:

How 'bout a blow-up doll? Got about three of those. Blonde, brunette or redhead. Half off, but you gotta choose which half."

Silence. Stone cold silence. I waited him out.

"So, no warsher then."

I died a thousand deaths.

"Uh, no," I croaked, clearing my throat and now desperately trying to make some sort of amends. "You might want to check with the Habitat store or the Hospice Barn. They often have appliances."

"I'll do that," he replied, gratefully. "I thank you."

And then, just as I was putting down the phone …

"Good luck with them dolls."

Pam Banana

At the risk of sounding 5 years old: "I never win any-thing!"

Which is why, with bated breath, I have waited for my telephone to ring at precisely 1 p.m. on Saturdays, the exact time in which my local feed store, The Hayrack, has been holding a weekly drawing for five bags of horse feed to those who have deposited tickets into a glass bowl with each store purchase. With the extra expenses caused by the drought and added freight charges slapped onto everything we are purchasing, receiving five free 50-pound bags of horse feed is like winning the lottery.

Because I have zero storage at my barn - it's stuffed to the rafters with horses - I find it necessary to make several trips to The Hayrack each week. You'd think that by now, surely my tickets would simply overwhelm anyone else's and I would be the grand-prize winner. Well, the only prize winner. But it is not to be. For two Saturdays now, I have glowered at my silent, sullen telephone with the same expression that a frustrated wife stares at her non-communicative husband who reads the newspaper at the breakfast table.

I never win anything!

That is not entirely true. I did win a raffle at a local Dollar Store. It was terribly exciting: The big prize was "The Windstream 500," a big box fan that could stand on its own. I thought, "This will be terrific in the aisle of the barn to help keep the horses cool!"

As I filled out my raffle card, I saw that I was obliged to write my name and phone number. I hesitated. Being a minor celebrity with a radio show, one does have, sadly, to think about security in this age of stalkers and senseless crime.

Should I really put down my legal name and home phone number? It nagged at me and I had a sudden, inspired flash of brilliance and thought, "Well, I shall just make up a false last name and who shall be the wiser?" Not a bad idea, really, had I chosen "Pam Smith" or "Pam Johnson."

I chose "Pam Banana."

You can imagine the thrill that leapt into my heart as the phone jingled promptly a day later and I was informed that I, Pam Banana, was the lucky winner of the Windstream 500!

With a giddiness I haven't felt since finishing second-to-last in my third-grade field day 100-yard dash, I sped the dually down the street and arrived within minutes to claim my prize.

Clasping the enormous fan to my chest, I presented my winning ticket. The cashier, not looking up from her slightly chipped crimson fingernail, mumbled, "I need to see your identification."

"Certainly!" I chirped, pulling out my driver's license.

"That doesn't say 'Pam Banana,' " she replied.

"Well, no, but my actual last name is 'Stone.' I just made up 'Banana.' "

"Your identification has to match the raffle ticket, or I can't give you the fan," she said, flicking off another small bit of red varnish.

"I am Pam Banana, but my real last name is Stone," I explained again, looking nervously at the queue of customers that were waiting to check out. "Like I said, I made up the name. I mean, who the hell is called Banana?"

The cashier looked up, bored. "Well, evidently you are, but you can't prove it. Please stand to the side so I can check out these people."

I had reduced myself, a 40-year-old woman, to standing in a Dollar Store on a Thursday afternoon, hearing my own voice bleat pathetically, "But I am Pam Banana. I am!"

I never win anything.

Ears Looking At You

As far as mini-mules go, ours is rebellious and not terribly grateful, considering he's a rescue.

Two Fridays ago, as a muggy day was drawing to a close, Paul and I were bringing the horses in from the fields for dinner when Lionel, the mule, slipped between two big warmbloods and squeaked through the gate at a brisk trot. Having witnessed this ploy before it is not normally a matter of grave concern, as Lionel is usually only in a rude rush to get to his feed bucket and simply passes through the barn and into his tree-lined paddock.

This day, however, he made a sharp turn before reaching his usual destination and tore through the apple orchard without even sampling a few windfalls. In a flash, he descended into the woods and I heard my neighbor's dogs alerting the world that something red with enormous ears was in the vicinity.

Earlier, my sister had left an inviting message on our answering machine saying she was having my mother for tea, had baked scones and a cake and would I like to come over? Yes, I thought, stomping through the woods, stepping high with bare, scratched legs over the abundant poison ivy, I would. The thought of being freshly showered and cool, sitting in her charming little house and sipping from her best china was an idyllic one that couldn't possibly have been realized in my state of sweat and fury as I made the steep descent to where the woods spill out into acres of corn fields.

Between splutterings of "Stupid mule!" and "I should just leave you out all night!" I would occasionally catch sight of rumpled leaves and droppings that could only have been deposited by something not quite 11 hands in height, giving me clues that Lionel was following the same path. Standing at the lip of the corn field, my attention was drawn to three tree stands, making the hair on my neck rise until I quickly remembered deer season hadn't officially begun. Having no clue to where my prey could be, I plunged straight into the corn, which, at this stage, was nearing 4 feet high, wondering if I would come across any dead baseball players or, as a consolation, a mule. The earth was still damp from a recent rain, and before long appeared the distinct, tiny hoof prints that led me on an interesting maze of circles and right angles. Shaking the feed scoop I had brought, I called, "Lionel ..." in a low voice which he blatantly ignored. But he was betrayed by the tips of his ears rising above the corn.

"You wretched, wicked beast!" I scolded, snapping the lead rope to his halter and hauling him back up the hill into the woods where we were feasted upon by deerflies and mosquitoes. We took the long way around so that I could apologize to my neighbor for the ruckus and ended up at the top of their driveway where I was met by Paul in his Honda.

Noting my glare, he quickly lowered the driver's side window and from the air-conditioned comfort within, bleated, "I was just coming to look for him!"

"Yes," I retorted, jerking open the car door, obliging him to step into the street and take charge of Lionel. "Everyone knows mules stick to the main road." With that, I drove off in a huff, leaving man and mule in the middle of the road. It wasn't a kind thing to do, of course, but I was late for tea.

Keep Your Pants On

"David's coming over around two," said Paul, popping his head into the office. "Make sure you have pants on."

Probably not the sort of statement you would expect to hear within a family household on a hot, June afternoon. However, for those of us without children, not only would it be commonplace, it might just be the norm.

"I will," I replied, as Paul walked back down the hall clad only in his boxers.

It occurred to me, arriving home and still dressed from grocery shopping, that perhaps most of the world's problems, and certainly marriages, could be repaired if only more people were able to lounge comfortably in their underclothes.

"Can you imagine what it must be like," I said to Paul later that evening, beer in hand, television on mute during a commercial showing a harried mother dealing with a house filled with screaming children. "To work hard all day in a suit, deal with an awful commute home, and then when you actually get home, because you have kids, you have to remain dressed? You could never just walk around in your underwear, and really, people desperately need to walk around in their underwear."

"Yes," Paul nodded. "Even putting on shorts and a tank top just isn't the same."

It's one reason I love our farm. We are set far from the road and shrouded in the complete privacy of oaks, poplars and acres of fields. If inclined, one could walk around naked, which is probably why UPS refuses to deliver to us anymore.

But hiccups can occur. If I were to point out the main difference between my former life in Los Angeles and the one now in a town of 2,000, I'd have to say that in a small town, people just show up. Particularly this time of year, they stand beaming in front of the storm door with a grocery bag filled with home-grown squash or tomatoes, or, like one recent morning, knocking hopefully, looking for handyman-type work.

Standing behind the kitchen island, pulling a coffee cup out of the cabinet, I was jolted by this sudden knock and spun around to look across our open-plan room directly into the eyes of this fellow, standing behind the glass door.

"Didn't mean to scare you!" he called, touching the brim of his baseball cap. "I'm just driving around the neighborhood looking for odd jobs."

"Tell ya what," I called back, pantless, from behind the safety of the island. "Go around back and my husband's in the vegetable garden. Ask him."

He touched the brim of his cap once more and as soon as I heard him clomp down the front steps, I dashed to the mud room and threw on a pair of jeans. No sooner had I buttoned them up then I heard his truck start and, surprised, saw him turn around and disappear back up the drive at a rapid clip.

Within moments, Paul entered, towel wound around his waist, straw hat still sheltering his head. "Who was that?" he asked.

"You didn't see him?" I replied, adding carefully, "What have you been doing?"

"Weed-eating around the vegetable beds. When I was done, I was so hot and sweaty that I just hosed off outside."

"With your hat still on?"

"A gentleman only takes off his hat for a lady," he said, removing it with a flourish. "Why do you ask?"

"Well, he clearly saw you."

"Ah," Paul said, grabbing a pair of shorts and heading upstairs. "Then next time I'll make sure I take two hats!"

A Terrier's Touch

At the end of each long, hot, summer day, the house would have to be fully engulfed in flames to dislodge me from the sofa.

Paul and I spend the majority of our life outdoors: he at the nursery and me riding, teaching and emptying many a wheelbarrow into the manure pile.

We think of 6 p.m. as the cocktail hour: a chilled glass of wine for me, a martini for him, and Brian Williams with his understanding, sympathetic eyebrows giving us the evening news. Bone-tired, from here we scratch up something resembling dinner (this has been known to be chips and salsa or a hard boiled egg), watch a couple of favorite programs and fade into sleep, arms filled with dogs.

But animals have cunning ways to tempt their self-appointed masters into the great outdoors. Rosie, in particular, getting stronger each day from her recent illness, snuffled onto my chest during a commercial and unapologetically gave me a whiff of something utterly vile she had apparently rolled in when I let her out to do her business a few minutes earlier.

"Ugh..." I groaned, pulling myself upright on the sofa and, like many a stupid person who, when smelling something horrid, put my nose to her neck to smell it again. It was foul and at the same time Paul began sniffing about Bonnie's torso only to confirm that both dogs had rolled in the droppings of something that clearly wasn't a vegetarian.

"We're going to have to take them to the barn and give them a bath in the wash rack." I sighed, lifting Rosie, looking very pleased with herself, and departing through the mudroom door.

It was one of those magically rare summer evenings when a front moves through from the north and the stifling heat of the day suddenly lifts, cooling the air deliciously with strong breezes amid a spectacular sunset settling over a mackerel sky. Both dogs were scrubbed and rinsed clean and, as dogs do, immediately rolled with abandon in the grass.

Too invigorated to go back indoors, we took the girls into the fields, freshly mown and intoxicatingly sweet, to watch the culmination of the sunset while the wind played over the tops of the oaks and kept insects in the next ZIP code. I have rarely seen such colors: first rose, then orange ebbing into a silvery lavender ... however, the most heartswelling sight was to see Rosie overtake Bonnie as they tore through the field below, ears flying, tongue flapping, eyes radiant with health and vitality. As long as I live, I shall remember the scene.

"That," I said, turning to Paul. "was worth every penny that went to the vet bill." He agreed, and we stood at the top of a hill and watched the hijinks for several more minutes before turning back home in the gathering dark.

It's shameful how we can almost miss a wondrous moment owing to sedentary habits. Sometimes nature is forced to step in and shake us by the shoulders to remind us we're given very little time, really, to experience the wonders of her palette. She does this with fireflies and rainbows, lightning and snow, and every now and then, if need be, something particularly disgusting on the neck of a terrier.

Fine China

Anyone who knows me would declare that I am not the least prudish (20 years of touring as a stand-up comic would bulldoze that assumption) but, every now and then, a situation arises which is rather awkward.

Recently, I was asked to appear, for charity, in the theatrical production of the, er …well, let's just leave out the first word and state the second: "Monologues." If you're a man reading this and are now frowning, ask your wife. If you're a child reading this, firstly, good for you for spending five minutes away from your "Killzone 2," and secondly, go eat your vegetables.

The "Monologues" was something I agreed to when my radio co-host, Sharon, not only the daughter of a Baptist preacher but is also a minister herself, had to pull out at the last moment owing to a scheduling conflict (so she says) and my other co-host, Ramona, promised me that my, er, "character," would get to be "the proper one."

"Is the proper one a good one?" I asked.

"Oh, yeah!" she enthused. "I've got the worst one -- mine's hostile from having been abused."

Oh.

The most difficult part, I feared, was informing my mother when she asked what I was doing the following Saturday.

"Well, actually, I'm going to Winthrop University to do a sort of play," I replied, immediately turning my back to her and busying myself about the kitchen.

"That's nice," she mused. "What sort of play?"

Before I go any further, it's important to point out that my mother is 89 years of age, survived the Blitz in London and drinks sherry every afternoon at 5 p.m.

"It's really not a play because we don't really interact. It's a few of us ladies all reading from specific scripts ..."

"What's it called?"

This is where being Southern is an enormous help. My mind flashed to all the very delicate ways that Bible-belt ladies refer to things.

Once, when a particular blue-blooded Charlestonian told me she was having "female problems," I asked, "What? You can't parallel park?" But this would require something far more imaginative.

Suddenly, a story that Sharon had recently shared came to the rescue.

"This lady I know just wouldn't say that word," she had explained, gulping with laughter, "so, instead, she would say -- "

"The Fine China Monologues," I said to my mother, turning round and resting my elbows on the kitchen counter.

"How very odd," she said, stirring her tea. "There's a play very similar to that, called - "

Don't say it!

Donkey Konged!

When we took in our latest rescue, Teddy, we surmised from a tattered copy of "Donkeys for Dummies" that these satellite-eared equids are somewhat renowned for being territorial.

This is why farmers often keep one on their property; they are absolutely lethal to coyotes: charging, ears pinned back, nostrils flaring while their hapless prey bounds for its life out of the field and off to the next county.

What I didn't know was that a donkey will not tolerate anything in its domain. The first victim was Bonnie, our 10-year-old Jack Russell who, minding her own business, was busily digging after a vole in the deep grass very near the fence.

While leading a horse in from the field I saw a brown, shaggy flash out of the corner of my eye and, in horror, realized Teddy was after Bonnie. I screamed for her attention but too late — Teddy charged completely over her but, somehow, (perhaps on purpose?) not a single hoof touched her. Scampering away, shaking from head to tail, Bonnie learned a profound lesson in respect and now refuses to even enter the field unless carried in my arms.

Rosie, our one-eyed rat terrier, also a rescue and chronically disobedient, ignored my calls of warning and trotted happily through enemy territory as I hacked back the honeysuckle that was devouring my fence near the roadway, a good 10 acres from the house.

Teddy, who up to that point had been curiously observing my work, flicked one ear back and turned his head slowly, not unlike a periscope searching for enemy ships among the fescue. In a flash, he spun around on his hindquarters and galloped across the grass, head down, eyes locked and loaded on Rosie who, eye bulging with fear, turned, yelping, and took off at full speed.

All I could do was channel Peter Falk from "The In-Laws" and bellow, "Serpentine, Rosie, serpentine!"

And she did! Rosie hurtled down the hill, running a graph of peaks and valleys like the tech market in the 1990s, spinning twice around a tulip poplar tree and, with the fence to the driveway approaching, flattened her dappled body and slipped beneath the bottom rail with Teddy's bared teeth inches from her backside.

Unlike Bonnie, Rosie now lives to antagonize the donkey and purposely strays into his path — but only if an escape route is within sight.

"If this behavior continues," I said cautiously to Paul who, taking a break from mowing, was lovingly combing out Teddy's tail, "we're going to have to find a home for Teddy. He's being really aggressive with the dogs."

"They're known to be," Paul replied, scratching Teddy's ears. "Let's give him a chance; he's only doing his job. The dogs need to learn a bit more respect."

But it wasn't just dogs.

One morning, well into my zone of stall-cleaning (it's amazing how many problems are solved during the rhythm of scooping and raking), I took note of both my horses, turned to their respective windows, alert and snorting at something catching their eye in the field.

What sounded like someone tuning up a set of bagpipes turned out to be Teddy aggressively herding an infuriated herd of wild turkeys down through a dried creek bed and into the woods.

The lone male, giving a last-ditch show of bravado before his girls, turned to swell his chest while fanning out his tail feathers, which was like a red flag to a bull. Teddy surged forward and took a formidable chomp, resulting in a mouthful of feathers and a shrieking Tom Turkey who disappeared from view.

"He's chasing turkeys now," I mentioned later that evening to Paul.

"Maybe he thought they were dangerous to the property," Paul suggested, defensively. "I mean, they could be full of rabies or something."

"You sound like Casey Anthony's mother!" I said, exasperated. "At some point you have to see he's not the sweet little Eeyore you think he is."

It wasn't until the following week, when I squinted my eyes to take in the sight of an orange blur tearing across the front pasture — seemingly without touching the ground — that even Paul began to have second thoughts.

"He's got Dennis up a sweet gum tree and won't let him down," I said casually, coming into the kitchen for a coffee. "You'll need a ladder."

"Dennis? He's got Dennis?" Paul gasped in alarm, the prospect of his favorite cat being in peril leading him to dash out the door.

Acres away, Dennis' fate was spared by Teddy catching sight of two squirrels, thrilled by the absence of the terriers, gamboling around the trunk of nearby oak. Like a predator drone, Teddy changed targets and Dennis launched himself from his perch and bounded the last few feet to the safety of the driveway, twining himself around Paul's legs as he met him halfway, ladder over his shoulder.

Minutes later, I heard the unmistakable sound of hammer and wood.

"What are you doing?" I asked, watching Paul pound a sign into the ground near the house.

"Best security system we've ever had," he said proudly, standing back to show me his hand-lettered endeavor which read,

"Forget the dogs, beware of donkey!"

Battered and Dipped

Here's the deal: If you're a woman, particularly in the South, sporting any sort of facial injury, it's immediately assumed that a guy's decked you.

How sexist is that?

And if you're built like me, towering over 6 feet and composed of angular knees and elbows, you are nearly always smacking into something. I have created enormous lumps on my hip bone from not clearing the corner of the kitchen island in the middle of the night and actually shattered a light fixture in the bathroom with my hand when, not thinking, I extended my arm sharply upward while blow-drying the back of my hair.

But none of these prepared me for a recent experience after I was nipped on the forearm by a horse, resulting in a massive blue-back bruise on my bicep and catching the side of my cheek on the same day with the chrome snap of a lead rope (don't ask — I couldn't do it again if you paid me a million dollars).

So, relatively used to appearing like a bruised apple, I didn't hesitate to ride with Paul over to Tractor Supply to price some electric fans for the barn and replace something that had snapped on the bush hog.

Standing in line at the cash register, I became aware of two pairs of eyes taking stock of my exposed arm and face. As the women glanced at me and then each other, their eyes narrowed as they at last rested upon their hapless target: Paul, who began to feel a touch uneasy.

"You battering bully!" glared one pair of eyes.

"Abusive jerk!" said another.

Paul, now distinctly feeling this unjust accusation, mumbled to me, "Come stand by me"

You'll have to forgive me for what I did next. Once a stand-up comic, always a stand-up comic, and the temptation to throw your partner under the bus is simply too delicious to resist.

"OK," I said, quivering, and flung up an arm as if to ward off an incoming blow.

"Stop that!" he said, horrified. "Stop!"

"Oh ..." I repeated. "OK. Sorry honey!" And continued to feign my act through check-out and all the way across the parking lot.

"I am never, ever, going back to that store," Paul fumed, firing up the truck. "Ever. I hope you're satisfied. That stuff is nothing to joke about!"

He's right. It is nothing to joke about. And I'll never do it again.

Well ...

Bathing Beauty

For the third time this year, I have been challenged in the most disgusting manner by a temperamental septic tank that takes fiendish delight in greeting Paul and me with three inches of your worst nightmare bubbling up in our bathtub.

Living on a farm with an array of critters, I have long ago abandoned the romantic ideal of bucolic country life and embraced the less than "soft-focus" reality.

Having cats means that, not infrequently, I am awakened in the wee hours by the retching sound that one learns to immediately recognize as a fur ball. You quickly learn that you have only three "aacks!" before this particular gift appears on the carpet.

A dog that begins stretching its neck while opening and closing its mouth is the unmistakable warning to remove the animal immediately to the front yard.

And lifting a horse's hind leg in order to clean out its hoof is the equine equivalent to playing "Pull my finger."

Rustic life means you willingly sacrifice the modern conveniences of your cosmopolitan friends.

We have no garbage service in our area and, while I'd like to say we drive our refuse weekly to the recycling center, the truth is we tend to put it off until our bins are overflowing onto the mudroom floor.

Because we shudder at the thought of living near any big-box stores, we happily drive the forty minutes to a Home Depot in the rare event we can't find what we need at our local hardware store.

However, I would never have called our existence primitive until Paul and I realized that our septic tank's vicious sense of humor of backing up on a Saturday would prevent us from either washing a load of laundry or, indeed bathing, until the plumber could be summoned on the following Monday.

Most of us can "get by" if we must with a quick wash around the edges for a day, but when you have horses, by the time evening rolls around and you have mucked stalls, fed, ridden, cleaned tack and unloaded a truckful of hay, you positively reek, and the superficial swipe with the wash cloth will simply not suffice.

Suddenly, the wash rack in front of my barn - a concrete affair with tall wooden pillars on either side to cross tie a horse as he is bathed from the garden hose - looked positively delicious.

In the early evening air, privacy secured by the massive oaks and acres of grass before me, I had the most marvelous shower I have had in years: a soft, autumnal light slanted across the fields and a breeze played amid the tops of the trees.

Like a shot, a cardinal swept past and alighted atop a fence post.

Patting down with my sun-warmed towel and changing into my evening attire of T-shirt and gym shorts, I walked back to the house with a newfound appreciation for the world and my place within it.

The septic tank will, it is hoped, be repaired come Monday, along with a scouring of the tub unmatched by even Hazmat.

But until the weather gets much colder or I accidentally surprise the FedEx man, I just might not use it.

State Fair

Last year, Paul indulged me in a dream that has been gnawing inside for years.

A baby? Please — I nipped this family tree in the bud years ago. Hacked it down, paved it over. Quite enough dysfunction, thank you very much.

Another horse? I'd get that without even mentioning it to Paul.

No, I'd been hankering (did I actually say "hankering"?) to go to a state fair for years. Years. The last time was in Georgia, when I was about 14. My father took my best friend, Jennifer, and me and I'll never forget that when we asked Jennifer's mother which stuffed animal we should try to win for her, she actually said, "A snake."

Who requests a snake?

Anyway, believe it or not, Jennifer managed to toss three pennies inside three glass jars atop a wooden table and, behold, there was an enormous, 10-foot-long snake, wrapped around the tent pole, there for the taking. It was black with green spots and a hissing, purple felt tongue.

We felt triumphant as we strolled through the midway, the snake wrapped around our shoulders. We decided the snake, named for alliteration's sake, Sam, should accompany us on every ride. My father, looking at his watch every four minutes, was prodding us to hurry, so we only rode about three rides before we were hustled back into his Impala and driven home, Sam's head hanging out the back window and his tail, having trailed behind us throughout the fairgrounds, covered in dust and chewing gum.

It was magic.

So when I saw the ads proclaiming the North Carolina Mountain State Fair was coming to Fletcher, N.C., my mind spun backward to being 14, eating cotton candy, caramel apples and riding the Bobsled and Scrambler.

"Please, can we go, please?" I badgered Paul, who wanted nothing more than to relax on the couch and watch the first football games of the season. "I'll drive. I'll pay for all the rides. I'll buy the food!"

He looked at my breathless expression for a long moment. "What are you, five?" he asked.

It worked. There we were, standing in line, buying tickets. Not bad: five bucks to get in. We strolled around the livestock, admiring cows and goats, and saw a terrific demonstration of a Border collie working sheep.

From there, the midway beckoned: flashing lights, sirens, blaring music and lots of people who showed excessive amounts of tattooed flesh. I was going to ride everything.

Rearing before us in all its garish glory was the Bobsled. We were ushered into our swinging "sled," the rock music exploded and Paul found it a good time to say, "Keep in mind that all these rides are designed to break down easily to be shoved into the back of a truck and driven to the next gig. There's probably 12 bolts missing."

With that, the Bobsled swung into action, whirling us round and round at a furious pace, bouncing over "moguls" and squashing me into Paul, clinging to the bar.

"Ow," I said.

"What?" he yelled.

"OW! My neck hurts!" The G-force was really straining as I fought not to smash the sides of our heads together.

After an eternity, the Bobsled slowed. And stopped. And to my absolute horror, began to repeat its cycle. Backwards.

It's an awful thing to realize, in a crushing moment, one's limitations. I'm not 14. I'm a middle-aged woman with a stiff neck. All I wanted was to get the hell out of there. Paul bought me a slice of pizza and a soft-serve ice cream and my mood lightened somewhat.

"Let's ride the Ferris wheel," he suggested. "The sun's just setting behind the mountains and we'll get a beautiful view."

The wheel took us into its care and delivered us carefully and slowly to the top, where it paused to give us the sight of a blazing sun descending behind the blue wall.

"I think this is more your speed," Paul said, patting my knee.

I nearly pushed him out. Stiff neck and all.

A Tribute To Moose

Oftentimes, we read poignant, endearing, tales of the cherished animals in our lives only after they have departed and left us bereft of comfort and daily companionship.

Because of this, I refused to read 'Marley and Me,' John Grogan's account of the boisterous relationship with his much-adored Labrador, because I knew it would take me days to get over it.

Even James Herriot's collection of "Cat" and "Dog Stories" had heartbreaking moments within the humor and charm. The loss of our own pets is painful enough - I simply cannot read about others, especially when the authors have done such an effective job of utterly captivating us in the first few chapters when the animal is young and full of life.

Last Sunday, I walked out as usual at 6 a.m. to feed our four horses and mini-mule. My heart went to my throat as I approached the paddock behind the barn and saw through the trees the enormous, white, body of my oldest, a 29-year-old Percheron-cross gelding, Moose, down on his side. Normally waiting bright-eyed by the gate, he is the first to whinny impatiently for his breakfast, a nano-second before his mule companion, Lionel, wakes the neighborhood with a series of shuddering brays. He now lay on the damp ground, coat clammy with dried sweat and wild-eyed.

I have owned Moose for 27 years. He was a slaughter-house rescue that was purchased for barely more than the price of his weight in meat. I had no money and he had little hope. Severely abused and malnourished, it wasn't long before his sunken flanks filled out and the summer sore on his hock disappeared. However, regardless of a long, loving, and patient relationship, he has never completely lost his fear of humans. He deeply distrusts most men and, to this day, will fling his head in fear of a beating if one moves too quickly around him.

Training Moose was both a pleasure and an adventure: he took comfortably to the saddle and bridle and had a lovely work ethic. Genuinely trying to please, in all our years together, it never occurred to him to offer a buck or a kick. On his fourth ride, he suggested we try a canter in an enormous, open, field, which began as a great success. Anyone witnessing the event would have seen an ebullient pair cantering steadily along the track and disappear in one, sideways body-leap into the woods, only to resurface, five minutes later, scratched and covered with leaves and twigs, calmly resuming the task at hand.

Moose was like that - you could ride him past a bucket or a chair 40 times and on the 41st time, he behaved as if he had seen it for the first time, insisting that it housed a tiger, and in one motion, would spin and bolt, which proved to be most unseating. It was never with malice and, if anything, taught me to be a better and more attuned rider.

The time came for our first competitions together. While considered a "backyard horse," meaning, an animal meant more for trail or pleasure riding rather than being braided and shown against gleaming Thoroughbreds, Moose presented me with an ability I have always been breathlessly grateful for: Each time we rode before a judge, regardless if he had just been spooky or nervous in the warm-up area, he would give me the ride of my life. Because of this, we won each horse trial entered in his fifth year. The corner hutch in my kitchen is littered with faded blue ribbons and photographs showing him galloping enthusiastically during his "honor round."

When I moved to California from Georgia in 1985, Moose followed a year-and-a-half later. Here he blossomed further: his three correct gaits earned him a hatful of awards in dressage shows and handed me the most exciting cross country round I've ever ridden. He was boarded for a time in Malibu, where his view of the Pacific was much better than my view of the brick wall of an alley behind my apartment in Hollywood.

When seasonal wild fires broke out, he was one of the last horses evacuated from the ranch, as there was a shortage of trailers. Our neighbor across the street, none other than the actor and horseman, Tom Selleck, offered a Quarter Horse-sized stock trailer that Moose, massively built and much taller than a Quarter Horse, refused to climb into.

"Are you insane?" I barked, smacking him on the rump, "This is Tom Selleck's trailer! Get in there!" Sighing, he clambered aboard and lowered his head so as not to smack the ceiling.

When I'd had enough of Los Angeles and returned to the south in 1999, Moose, long retired, traveled in an enormous van with my other two competition horses and began his autumn years in the oak-shaded fields of our farm in the Upstate of South Carolina. While I was worried about the stress on an older horse from such a trip, Moose unloaded without incident, still munching his hay and looking with interest over his new digs.

After calling the vet that early Sunday morning, I sat cross-legged in the paddock as it lightly rained and pulled his head onto my lap. As I stroked his face, he lipped my palm with his muzzle and his eyes asked me why he couldn't get up.

Dr McDaniel arrived, pulled out of both his retirement and warm bed by my tearful plea, listened to Moose's stomach and declared him to have colic. Whether that came on first, which brought him down trying to escape the pain, or was the result of being down and unable to rise, we don't know. In his life, Moose has never been sick, ever. What we did know was that his expression was full of fire and fight. He wanted to get up and he didn't have that vague, tired, look of surrender. It took three attempts to get him to his feet. Enlisting Paul for extra help, Moose gave two mighty efforts, straining against the lead held fast by two strong men, and failed each time, crashing through the fence. Just as I was on the verge of saying, "Enough..." he heaved himself upon all fours and stood quaking, but secure.

Each passing minute brought recovery and strength. Dr. McDaniel, who has known Moose for years, commented his color was good and while he couldn't guarantee it wouldn't happen again, proclaimed him "one strong horse." As I write this, I can see my horse through my studio window, contentedly finishing his dinner and taking an irritated bite out of Lionel's mane as the mule tries to steal the last mouthful of grain in his feed tub. I don't know how many days or years I will be able to look upon this same scene, but I felt he deserved to have his story told while still here for me to read it to him.

AUTUMN

Halloweenies

In the 11 years that I have lived here, I have yet to see a single trick-or-treater come to my door.
Not one.

At first, I thought perhaps parents had finally woken to the fact that what is gleefully allowed on Halloween rather flies in the face of responsible child rearing: encouraging one's flesh and blood to go into the night with other children to unfamiliar homes and take candy from complete strangers who, like paying off the mob for protection, bow to extortion for the fear of an egg or toilet paper retaliation.

Then a friend of mine pointed out the obvious.

"Well, good Lord, look at the length of your driveway!" she exclaimed. "What kid is going to walk down that?"

It should be said that my driveway is an unpaved tenth of a mile long. There are no lights to guide one's way, and the house cannot be seen from our quiet country street.

What's creepier, more fun than that?

"Are you telling me that kids won't walk a few feet nowadays?" I replied, incredulous.

"Course not," she snorted. "Parents drive kids through neighborhoods they know and wait for them in the car. Nobody walks anymore. Particularly to your house."

That stung because my house is known, by my neighbors, the FedEx guy and pretty much everyone else in the general area except, evidently, the Realtor who sold it to me, as "The Crock Pot House." This is because the previous owner, an alleged drug dealer with a shady reputation and even shadier contacts, was found dead in the hot tub on the upstairs deck after being reported missing for more than five days.

Yes, the hot tub was on the entire time.

No, of course it's not still there.

I don't know if there is a ghost, but Paul and I decided if we see one, we'll call him Stew.

At any rate, this gives me another fine opportunity to shake my bony finger and point out another smug difference between my childhood and "these kids today."

For heaven's sake, what better destination on a dark Halloween night than apprehensively walking, giggling and shrieking with your friends toward a true "Boo Radley"- type residence in the middle of the country — down a pitch-black driveway that goes forever, flanked by trees in which roost owls?

And to top it off, a guy died there!

But just in case some of you kids have now decided to visit my "Little Crack House on the Prairie," be forewarned: I'm a bit of a "foodie" who shuns both red meat and poultry and thinks corn syrup and aspartame run through the veins of Beelzebub, so don't think you're going to get any tooth-rotting treat from me.

You'll be given a nice tuna sandwich on whole wheat, and you'll be grateful.

Or I'll send Stew to follow you home...

Even Better Than Pumpkin Spice!

It's not the sort of thing one brags about, but I sort of look forward to going to my local gas station/mini mart around this time of year.

They have one of those ubiquitous cappuccino machines that you stick a Styrofoam cup beneath and press a button for it to be filled to the top. Only in autumn do they stray from the usual French vanilla and hazelnut and offer "pumpkin spice."

I live for this.

"You're crazy," a friend admonished when I confessed my craving. "I got some kind of stomach bug from one of those machines. They never clean the insides of those things, you know."

As much as I'd like to think of myself as a maverick for
shrugging off the potential of E. coli, the truth was it had
been a lousy day: a chilly, wet, day that arrived with a
dishwasher that decided to flood the kitchen floor and the
subsequent breaking of a favorite plate upon unloading the
machine. Sticking a few bucks of "regular" in the Honda as
I stood shivering under the gas station canopy, I did what
most Americans do when depressed: went in search of
something to shove into my mouth.

I'm normally a tea drinker. With milk and no sugar, please.
But the stainless steel top of the cappuccino machine,
emblazoned with a pleasing illustration of a steaming,
frothy, drink, lured me toward it not unlike Donald
Sutherland approaching his girlfriend in the remake of
"Invasion of the Body Snatchers."

Securing my eco-hostile Styrofoam cup with its lid, I took
a long pull of the drink and felt a little better. I could taste
nutmeg somewhere within the hot liquid but, essentially,
I was freebasing a box of "Dixie Crystals" and beginning to
get a deserved headache.

Standing in line at the cash register, the cashier, a pretty
brunette with sparkling eyes, looked past me to the equally
young woman standing just behind.

"I've been waiting for you to come in," she said, smiling.
"I've got some good news for you. I'm pregnant."

"Oh, my gosh!" the other girl squealed. "Are you sure?"

"Pretty sure," the cashier replied. "I wanted to tell you."

"I just want to do a happy dance!" her friend gasped. "I'm just so excited for you! Oh, I hope it's a girl — they're so much easier to buy for."

And suddenly, while at first feeling awkward and self-conscious caught between these two, giddy, Jack Russells, my depression vanished like a puff of smoke. I've never had a maternal urge, but I would imagine it's something akin to looking at kittens on local humane society websites and desperately wanting them all.

At any rate, my mood brightened immediately, and I was grateful that this young woman had chosen to share her intensely private news in front of the general public standing in line at a gas station. I actually even mumbled something like, "Well, isn't that great?" and "Is it your first?" Because it's just impossible, isn't it, not to get caught up in the excitement between two giggling Southern girls? Too bad we can't bottle this sort of mood-lifter and sell it. Call it something like, "Y'all, listen up!"

And it's ever so much better for you than pumpkin spice

Pastoral Care

Since August, I'd like to say that I've been tremendously self-disciplined and have been going for a one-mile walk, twice a day.

I'd like to say that, but the truth of the matter is that I have a dear, older horse who suffered, back in July, an injury while playing about in the field and now requires a twice-daily walk to help knit the fibers of his torn tendon.

Unlike many of you lucky beasts who can, while cozily tucked up on the couch in your favorite sweats, look into the yearning eyes of your dog and say, "OK, I know you need to do business, but it's cold and we are only going right outside the door!" Fozzy and I must make these walks in all weather.

With the fawn-colored light that is particular to October streaming over the fields, still green and tender with grass, Fozzy and I have had some splendid talks, some meaningful silences, and, quite often, some heartfelt prayers.

Prayer feels natural in the early morn as we amble along the fence line and note the clouds tinged with tones of rose and gold, filigreed by the first rays of the sun. My shoes are quickly drenched by the dew-soaked grass, and Fozzy, alert and full of beans, snorts within the rhythm of his stride, his breath steaming out in twin, faint clouds that dissipate behind us.

This time of prayer feels very pure. Instead of the rote "God bless Mom and Dad ..." there is, rather, a heart-swelling feeling of thankfulness and peace. A sort of merging of earth and soul and truth and sky. Along these undulating hills and tree-skirted fields, for once I can actually be still — something that is quite impossible during the rest of the day — and absorb an enveloping sweetness, a security that eludes the half-hearted attempts I might normally make.

Our evening walk is different in that it tends to be a recap of the events of the day. A dilemma can generally be sorted out by the half-mile mark, and any discontent is quickly batted away by an appreciation of the beauty that surrounds us.

October means lazily soaping a leather rein while leaning against the tack room door and looking out over the farm, in no hurry whatsoever to go inside. It means stacking the year's last cut of hay and gathering the remaining windfalls in the apple orchard. It means not being lured by Facebook or e-mail but instead being tempted to clear wooded trails and take huge lungfuls of crisp, sharp air.

You would be wise to pay attention to your dog when he approaches you this evening for his walk. He knows something you don't.

Moving Mom

It is no exaggeration to say that I would rather have distended bowel than to move house.

And if we agree that moving oneself is a massive upheaval, then moving one's mother is something else entirely.

This past week, my mother, at age 89, has decided to "downsize" and move into a lovely retirement community. Because she is leaving a three-bedroom home for a one-bedroom apartment, draconian measures and cutthroat decisions, at least in her view, have been made.

"Now, Mom," I said, clearing out her chipped and faded everyday plates. "Surely you don't want to take any of this stuff with you."

"But I use them at lunch!" she cried, wounded.

"But you're taking only your very best furniture," I tried to reason. "I mean, you've got a Chippendale tallboys and a Sheraton writing desk. I just don't see packing a coffee mug with 'Carolina Alliance Bank' stamped across the front of it when you've got piles of Wedgewood."

"I like to have a little more than a cup of tea each morning, not too much, but just a little more. This mug is the perfect size."

The mug, I swear, smirked at me. It was then dutifully bubble-wrapped and set to the side.

"I'll get you, mug," I hissed, when my mother was out of earshot. "Just you wait."

The next task before me was the emptying of the massive tallboys in order to decrease its weight so that the movers, with perhaps the addition of performance-enhancing drugs, would be physically capable of muscling it out of the house onto the truck.

Working upward, I opened the first drawer and pulled out scads of ancient linens: hand-embroidered runners that hadn't seen the light of day since the Victorian era, a christening robe that had belonged to my grandmother in her infancy ... all these were carefully folded and removed. The second drawer contained more of the same and the third drawer was stuffed full of well-used and broken

Christmas decorations – red candles snapped in half, frayed ribbon, bits of moth-eaten felt.

"Ya gotta just motor through this stuff," I said, tossing most of the contents into a rapidly filling garbage bag at my side. My mother watched, incredulous of my speed. "Otherwise, we'll be here for weeks," I added, pulling open the fourth drawer, then hesitating.

Inside, carefully rolled and tied closed with ribbon, was every piece of artwork ever attempted by her children. Amateurish landscapes, hand-made birthday cards, and one which, in particular, stung.

It had been a pencil and watercolor wash I had done in the fourth grade of George Washington, resplendent in uniform, copied from an engraving within the Encyclopedia Britannica for a history project. Inheriting my mother's flair for illustration, it was quite well executed, and that had been the problem.

Hauled before the class, my teacher accused me of tracing the drawing and gave me an "F."

"But I didn't trace it!" I had cried. "I copied it, but I didn't trace it. The one in the book is only a few inches big – this one takes up the whole poster."

"No child can draw that well," said Mrs. Russell, flatly. "I can't draw that well. Take this note home to your mother explaining your grade and take your seat."

I will never forget the humiliation of being unfairly brandished a cheat over something that, only moments before, I had been so proud. The fact that my mother, once I returned home and seeing both the note and my fallen face, had telephoned the teacher in a fury to confirm my innocence, did little to soothe the wound that had been long forgotten until I opened the drawer.

"This," I said, rolling up George. "I think should be kept."

"Yes." Mom nodded. "You can put it next to the mug."

Men!

A friend of mine, heavily pregnant and overdue, shared with me (always a bad idea when one is always looking for ideas for a newspaper column) that when she was told by her doctor that if her baby didn't arrive very soon, she would need to check into hospital in a few days to help the process along at 6 o'clock in the morning, her husband said, "Well, what time do I have to be there?"

Oh, yes he did!

This story made me laugh out loud because I like her husband very much. He's a good guy who says, well, guy sorts of things. I truly don't think he meant to be insensitive; I think, like most men, he goes down the dreaded path of logic when his life partner, retaining water, miserable, sleep-deprived and fragile, very much needs to hear, "Then that's when we go, honey, and I'll be there holding your hand and rubbing your neck the whole time" and certainly not, "but what about the dogs?"

Paul tries very hard to be thoughtful. So much so that it can implode all around him.

When we lived in Los Angeles, Paul was installing roses at the estate of a supermodel, the exotically enchanting Cindy Crawford. And naturally, like a 5-year-old, I couldn't wait at the end of each day to ask whether he'd gotten a glimpse of the woman many of us would love to be mistaken for.

"Saw her today, as a matter of fact," he said, shrugging out of his sweatshirt on the way to the shower.

"What was she like?"

"Very nice … she was on her way to the gym and was very friendly."

"What was she wearing?" Because women always have to ask this.

Frowning, Paul replied, "I dunno, sweats — she had a baseball cap on."

"So her hair was pulled back in a ponytail?" I pressed further.

"I think," he said, trying to escape.

Standing in the door frame, blocking his departure, I popped the loaded question.

"And was she just knock-out, drop-dead gorgeous?"

An honest man, Paul croaked, "Yes," and then added, "if you like that sort of thing."

"And you don't?"

"Not really," he said, being utterly genuine. "I like you."

Trying to work that out in my head, I stepped aside, raised my hand and said, "Pass."

The truth is, we all say things on the spur of the moment that are never meant to be insensitive, and women are just as guilty as the men who are often regarded as clods, or at least I am.

"So, why are you wearing sunglasses in a nightclub?" I had asked one cowboy-hatted fellow who looked rather like Richard Petty and sat alone, right up front in the Austin comedy club, behind at least 10 empty Budweiser bottles.

"I'm blind," he said, and gestured to the sleeping guide dog beneath his chair.

You could hear a pin drop. And no back hoe available to help me dig myself out.

"Well, If that's all your beer, I hope he's driving!" I shot back, hopefully, and to my great relief, he leaned back his head and roared with laughter, followed by the rest of the audience, who had nervously held their collective breath. Chatting after the show, he actually said he enjoyed being picked out and treated like anyone else.

"Because when you look different," he explained, "people avoid you because they're scared they're gonna hurt your feelings. And all you want is to just be treated normal. You must know the feeling, being so freaky tall and all."

Oh, yes he did!

Praying For Peace

My radio co-hosts and I recently choreographed a special, two-hour episode to commemorate 9/11. We felt it important to include honoring the sacrifices of war with family members of those currently serving in our military, a discussion of bringing faiths together, and a Muslim guest who told us what it was like to be a Muslim both before and after the tragedy and what, in his opinion, would be an approach to cultivate peace and respect in the future.

Feedback regarding our Muslim guest after the show was overwhelmingly positive except for one listener, clearly angry in her tone displayed by the email she sent. While we remained respectful in our response to her, pointing out the violence also of those who killed countless numbers in the name of Christianity, I'm not sure we'll ever see eye to eye and I realize she is not alone in her condemnation of Islam in general.

While acknowledging the extremists that wish us harm, I can only reflect upon Muslims I have known personally: shopkeepers of which I was a steady patron in Los Angeles and a waiter in Las Vegas who, after frequent return engagements, became my rather close friend as he was always working the late shift that I took advantage of after my midnight show. I am always ravenous after a show. And it's got to be scrambled eggs with cheese and raisin toast. Don't ask me why. It's the only time I eat it, ever.

Mohammed and I discuss politics between decaf refills or when it's slow on the floor and he has a chance to talk. He shows me where he is able to commit to his praying, in a tiny alcove that houses the coffee machine and silverware. His prayer rug is rolled up and leans against the wall behind the door. It is touching. He is so spiritually evolved and intellectual that it is a constant challenge to keep up with him. What I can confirm is that his message is peace. Always. That what must be chosen is the ballot, not the bullet, and everyone in every country has a moral obligation to closely follow foreign policy and witness how it affects the world.

I haven't seen Mohammed in a couple of years. I don't even know if he still waits tables at Harrah's. I've been mostly home doing my radio job and teaching dressage.

When breaking news shows another day of indiscriminate violence and bloodshed somewhere in the world, I do send a fleeting thought his way and on Sundays, as I dress for church, my eyes linger over the delicate bracelet that he gave me as a gift when he returned from a trip to Egypt with his children. I had crumpled into the chair at my usual table, bleary eyed after performing three shows on a Saturday night to packed houses of people who had just lost their kids' college funds at the Craps Table, when he approached me with a tiny parcel. "I am so glad to see you again!" he said, placing the box next to my dinner plate. "I saw this on my visit and thought you would like it."

The bracelet is thin and plain with the exception of the engravings of the symbols of Christianity, Islam and Judaism, all entwined. It's not real silver and it was probably around five bucks. But it is one of the most valuable things I own.

With recent newscasts broadcasting arrests in terror plots and carnage foiled, I think, "Well Mohammed, I know we pray different prayers but certainly our prayers have been answered."

Guess Who's Not Coming To Dinner?

I'll bet everyone has, at one time or another, been asked that conversation starter: "So, if you could invite any six people, alive or dead, to a dinner party, who would you choose?"

The first time I was asked the question was by my fifth-grade teacher. It was a class assignment designed, I imagine, to make us think, discuss, compare and contrast.

Or, she was dying for a smoke in the ever so mysterious, hazy "teacher's lounge" and wanted to bail out of the class for 10 minutes.

I remember chewing on my pencil and pondering for about three minutes before writing down the name of a British show-jumper, the Beatles and Maria Rilke. The last entry, even I knew, was precocious, but I wanted to appear eclectic.

I was called upon first, recited my choices and sat down fairly smugly after correcting the teacher that Rilke was not a woman.

My smugness evaporated when the next child stood and quietly replied, "Jesus." Well, game over. She didn't even list another five, and I was mortified that I hadn't even considered Jesus. Of course, every other child, realizing their omission, quickly added Jesus to their list and their recitations sounded something like,

"Joe Namath, Mick Jagger, Jesus ..."

Recently, this dinner party query was asked of me again and, this time, I thought promptly to include Jesus at the top spot. The other five were nearly impossible to choose from a list of endless possibilities: Ghandi? Da Vinci? Edith Piaf? Churchill?

The one thing in common with which they would all be burdened, I supposed, was to have me as their rather lackluster host in my modest house with its pine floors in desperate need of refinishing.

Because an upcoming dinner party is when you look at your surroundings with despair, isn't it? You notice the dated decor of your kitchen or the bathroom faucet that needs replacing. The paint work behind the couch is scuffed and the carpets need to be steam cleaned.

Yes, it would be an embarrassment, would it not, to have Jesus over to dinner without an extreme makeover?

Wonder what he might say after that big, financial outlay as you gave him a tour of your sparkling new home. Surely he would be terribly impressed, wouldn't he, with your granite countertops and the walnut cabinetry and Viking range? And surely the money was well-spent on the massive wide-screen television in the new "media room," punctuated by the leather sectional?

And let's not forget the bathroom: the lavishly tiled floors leading to your dream garden tub.

Yeah, I'm embarrassed, too.

Think maybe those pine floors really aren't the biggest of my problems.

Faking Out Friends

It wasn't something I could put my finger on, but in the past couple of weeks I felt as if a couple of friends were behaving slightly different toward me.

Nothing negative, you understand, just wearing an expression of, for lack of a better word, concern.

With one, it began in my truck as I stopped to pump gas. I'd opened my purse to retrieve my debit card and we then returned to my house for lunch. She went from being chirpy and animated to far more quiet with a troubled brow. Nearly the same scenario was played out by another pal who had swung by to drop off some obligatory summer squash.

"You OK?" I asked, sliding a glass of iced tea toward her.

"Huh? Oh, yeah," she said after hesitating just a moment too long. Then, after an awkward silence she asked with false brightness, "You?"

"Me?" I replied. "Yeah, I'm fine. All good."

"Really?" she said, cocking her head and raising a carefully arched brow. "Are you?"

I couldn't contain a snort of laughter and said with mock seriousness, "Yes, I am really, really, fine. Why do you ask?"

Shaking her head she gave a wan smile, murmured she was glad I was fine and if I ever needed to talk, just to "give her a holler." From there she departed with one long, last look and swept down the front steps to her car.

"That was just the weirdest thing," I commented to Paul, coming in from the garden with more squash.

After relaying the story, Paul, as most men do over the dramas of the women in their lives, shrugged his shoulders and went back out.

A week later, when my other friend behaved in the same manner, I pounced.

"All right, what's up?" I demanded, snapping a bread stick like a pistol crack. "You're tip-toeing all around me!"

"Well," she said, looking down with sudden interest at an olive in her Greek salad. "I'm worried. I'm worried you're hiding something from me. You know you can tell me anything, Pam. If there's anything wrong with you …"

"What on earth are you talking about?" I cried. "Why do you think there's something wrong with me?"

Exasperated, she rose to her feet, walked to the kitchen counter and gestured with an elaborate flourish.

"These!" she said, pointing out eight small bottles of prescriptive medications. "And last week, when we were in your truck, I wasn't trying to look, but I noticed two more in your purse. I've never seen any medication over here before. All you've ever taken is vitamins. If you've become terribly ill, I just wish you'd share that with me!"

There are moments in life of which a comedian dreams. This was one. Wordlessly, I walked over to the counter, feigning illness, coughing, grasping the kitchen island for support and scooped up the bottleplans, shaking, placed them, one by one, into her hands.

"Oh, my gosh!" she gasped, her eyes beginning to brim with tears. "This is Enalapril — heart medication! And this is for acid reflux and this one's a strong antibiotic, and so is this one! And Novox — isn't that an anti-inflammatory?"

I nodded, and then unable to stifle a smile I whispered, "Read who they're prescribed to."

Her eyes widened and then reading aloud, the penny dropped, "Bonnie Stone and Vicki Zimmerman? Your dog? And the cat?"

I will laugh at that memory for the rest of my life. And the next time I need a big favor from someone I won't hesitate to line up those bottles in a place they're sure to be noticed.

Ain't folks nice when they think you're about to push up the squash?

Nuts

The weekend of my mother's 90th birthday could not have been more perfect: crisp air, lots of sun and jewel-toned leaves under which all the 'chillun' (as an old woman of my youth used to say), particularly, my great nephews and niece were playing.

The entire family had elected to make this birthday a sort of family reunion and it's safe to say that I haven't been surrounded by that many kids in quite sometime. Having considered bringing over a game, pumpkins to carve or a donkey to keep them occupied, I was delighted to see that these children, owing to very involved parenting, were completely natural (i.e., destructive) in the outdoor environment of my sister's farm: they climbed the pasture fence fearlessly in order to pat the necks of curious horses, they found large sticks and beat the ground, stabbed fallen leaves and each other.

Really, I thought, they're not terribly different from terriers. They have cheeky dispositions, can be awfully naughty, disobedient and often have things in their mouths requiring prompt removal. And, like terriers, they often need a firm reminder along with an instantly forgiving kiss and cuddle. All of this gave me an easy feeling of familiarity as I leaned against the deck railing talking to my niece, Courtney.

"Mom," called son, Grayson, from below.

"Hmmm?" Courtney replied.

"You know that metal thing that comes out the back of a car that if it's plugged up gets hot and explodes?"

This was not good.

"Yesss?"

"Well, " Grayson continued and pointed out the alleged perpetrators, all huddled around the back end of my truck. "They're stuffing black walnuts and rocks in it!"

Ye Gods!

In a flash, Courtney and I dashed down the front steps and the children, with the exception of the dimpled 4 yr old,

Oliver, who had his entire arm up the tail pipe, scattered like chickens to be queried by their mother, my other niece, Christy.

"Oliver," I said sternly. "Have you put anything up that pipe?"

A resolute shake of his golden curls was my only answer.

"I am so sorry," began Courtney, poking a stick up the pipe to dislodge any foreign bodies.

"Is it a breech birth?" I asked, and also began to dig.

After a few moments a lone, green-sheathed black walnut tumbled out.

Satisfied that no real harm was done, and after telling Oliver that he was very lucky that the tailpipe wasn't hot and how he could have been burned, or run over or had his arm stuck which would have resulted in a terrible surgery, he trotted away to throw an acorn at one of his brothers and we both gave the sigh and the roll of the eyes that precedes, "Kids!"

The rest of the day was uneventful. Everyone ate too much, my mother was photographed drinking three glasses of wine and blowing out her candles. As the shadows lengthened across the fields, children were corralled and preparations made for the drive back home to Georgia.

The following morning, eager to pick up a load of hay, I jumped in my truck and as I stepped on the brake before shifting into reverse, the pedal went straight to the floor taking my foot with it. With absolutely no ability to stop the vehicle, I called the garage and told them to expect a white Dodge to be brought in later on.

"Any idea what's wrong?" said Melissa, on the other end of the phone.

"Not sure." I replied grimly. "Just tell Jimmie to be on the lookout for walnuts."

Moonlight Ride

'Where are you?" I heard my sister ask upon answering the phone the other evening.

"Home," I replied into the receiver, frowning. "Why? Where are you?"

"At the end of the street, waiting for you."

"What?"

"I thought you said you wanted to go for a trail ride."

Glancing at the clock on the stove I laughed. "I meant during the day. It's 8 o'clock!"

"Precisely," she replied. "And there's a full moon and it's absolutely gorgeous out. Why don't you tack up and come along?"

Having one horse laid up from injury and another horse in training with me for which I was responsible, I was happy, in a cowardly way, to have an excuse not to participate.

"I'm in my jammies, I already rode this morning and, besides, can you imagine making that phone call?" I asked. "Sorry, but I'm afraid I broke your horse's leg riding at night and falling into a rabbit hole."

"Pfffft!" I could hear her dismiss my anemic concerns. "It's as bright as day outside. I'm now heading onto the trail and I'll be down at the bottoms if you change your mind."

The "bottoms" were a vast, flat area bordered by stream and woods used to grow corn and left fallow for the remainder of the year. It was a lovely area to go for a quiet walk or a bold canter and I thought of this as I hung up the phone, slightly deflated. It was as bright as day outside with a voluminous, full moon, and the night air was crisp and still.

I admired Katy for her brave ride into the night on her seasoned fox hunter and was grateful that she still clung to idea of adventure and romance that such a night was sure to give when so many of us, myself included, remain safely practical. There was a time when I wouldn't have hesitated and I remembered it well: swinging up, no saddle in place, onto the warm, round back of my little chestnut mare when I was around 17, finding the freshly cloaked fields of snow before me sparkling beneath the stars, irresistible. Crouching low over her neck, frozen hands clutching the reins deep within her wind-whipped mane, we cantered in utter silence the length of the field and walked steadily back, halting only once for me to slip to the ground at the gate and knock away the snow that had gathered in her hooves.

"I've always wanted to go for a moonlight ride and now I'm going to," were my sister's last words before she hung up. Prior to this I had mentioned I was glad she'd taken her phone along and she quipped that it really was of no use as there was no signal once deep into the woods.

Foolhardy, some would say. Asking for trouble.

Wish I'd gone.

Requiem For A Mini Mule

As a local farmer once put it, "If you're going to have livestock, you've gotta expect to have some deadstock, too."

This has been a season of loss for us here at the farm. And while I am not equating animals to humans, I'm beginning to understand my elderly mother who sighs and says, "Everyone I know is dying."

That, I have learned, is the price one pays for providing a "forever home" as we did for our ancient mini-mule, Lionel. Not particularly affectionate with those of the human variety, this tiny half-Shetland, half-donkey immediately latched onto another long-retired horse, my beloved draft-cross, Moose, who, at the time, was 26. Moose was most amenable, sharing his paddock with Lionel and tolerating his early morning brays which, like the clockwork of a rooster, occurred at 5 a.m.

Watching them wander through the fields together, staking out favorite trees from which they would enjoy shade and protection from flies, I often thought of them as Don Quixote and Pancho, exploring paths and marveling at the different wildlife that would appear from the cover of woods: wild turkeys, deer, even a bear. When Moose was put down three years later owing to a series of strokes and dramatic weight loss, Lionel adjusted to his loss by attaching himself to another dear elderly gelding, Scotty, whom we also lost this year at age 29.

Into his life appeared a glimmer of hope this spring, when I took into training a lovely bay 4-year-old named Dune, who became infatuated with Lionel as soon as their eyes met. Trying to keep Dune's attention while being worked in the arena became a challenge, as he was continually whinnying for his comrade on the other side of the farm, and he refused to eat his dinner if he could not see Lionel from the window of his stall.

As the French say, "In each relationship, there is one who kisses and one who is kissed." Clearly the kisser in this equine arrangement was Dune, and happy he was to oblige.

Two days ago, "colic weather," as we horse people call it, arrived: a sudden shift from hot, dry days to cool, wet weather can play havoc with the delicate systems of horses, and Lionel, now approaching 40, woke up with a stomach ache. The fear is always that a horse will lie down and roll to try and alleviate the pain and, in the process, twist an intestine — a condition that can only be corrected by immediate surgery of which Lionel, given his great age, was not a candidate. Finding him already down, I had no idea how long he had been in pain or how he had reacted.

Our vet responded to my 6 a.m. call by arriving promptly and administering painkilling drugs as well as inserting a tube down his throat into which she poured warm water and electrolytes, since he was dehydrated. Hoping his condition was caused by an impaction that would "pass," we walked him up and down the drive to no avail. Using an approach that had saved him from a similar bout years ago, he was attached to an IV drip of two fluid-filled 5-liter bags, which were to be emptied and then re-attached to two more, hoping we could flush him clean.

Nearly immediately, he went into deep distress, despite the painkillers, and the realization was immediate: The fluid had nowhere to go as the suspected twist made itself known. At 2 p.m., Lionel went down, our vet returned immediately, and injected him with a heavy sedative that prevented him from even being aware of the second and final shot.

Dune, turned out in the field, stood immobile against the fence rail, watching everything.

"It's going to be hardest on him," I said chokingly to Paul. "Perhaps he has a sense of what's happening and he'll understand it all."

To make sure, we led Dune carefully to Lionel's body, where he began to sniff and nuzzle. When this failed to elicit a response, he nipped his neck and shoulder. I hoped that would create a sense of closure for him, but I was wrong.

Dune ate his dinner that evening peering over his stall door with dismay toward Lionel's empty paddock. It wasn't until the following morning, when I turned him out into the field that he took off cantering the perimeter and calling repeatedly for his lost friend. As the morning broadened into afternoon, he settled and began to graze, periodically lifting his head and calling out with a low nicker. I tacked him up and we went for a ride, where we had a long talk about the "Rainbow Bridge" and I showed him where Lionel was buried, next to Moose, beneath their favorite oak.

Afterward, in the barn, Dune looked across the aisle to my other two horses for comfort and ate his dinner quietly because horses know, perhaps with more clarity than humans, that life indeed goes on.

WINTER

Small Fall, Big Question

"I wonder," I thought, pulling myself out of the slop in front of the manure pile beautifully cloaked in the snow of a recent winter storm, "how long it would take for Paul to come looking for me if I had really hurt myself just then."

It's a dicey scenario, trekking out to the barn before it occurs to the sun to rise on a dark January morning. The plummeting temperatures create a frozen crust atop the snow that gives a satisfying crunch while walking tentatively toward the horses, kept up for days in a row and now snorting in alarm at such a noise at such an hour.

Where I had dumped the manure was gloppy, with a sheen of ice beneath. Predictably, one muck boot was sent flying forward, and, while I didn't go down heavily, there was no grace involved as I crumpled down in a Carhart-attired angry heap.

There's nothing worse on a bitter morning than being cold and wet. And no one, save those convicted of war crimes, should experience the added humility of soaking manure to the mix.

It normally takes me just over an hour to feed, clean stalls, scrub and refill water buckets and sweep clean the aisle. On this morning, chores were taking well over an hour and a half, and it was nearly 8 a.m. before I crept back toward the house, noting the well-worn path was now packed with snow and frozen so hard that it resembled a luge track for terriers.

Paul was inside enjoying his second cup of tea and watching the sports wrap-up on ESPN.

The question I had asked myself in the barn began to fester a little but gave way to the rational acknowledgment that these horses weren't his, after all — not to mention that, like most horsewomen, I'm self-sufficient to the extent of being a control freak.

So why should it have occurred to him to perhaps pop his head out the mudroom door and call out just to make sure I hadn't slipped and was slowly losing my life, owing to an aneurysm?

Sitting down in the office and pulling up my Facebook page, I asked the same question to all my horsey "friends":

"How long would it take for your husband to come check on you in the barn to see if you're OK?"

Misery indeed loves company, and within minutes I was flooded with replies:

"How long? Heck, he wouldn't even notice!"

"Probably come spring."

"When the stench became too strong to ignore."

Chuckling softly to myself, I left the computer, padded into the kitchen and switched on the electric kettle.

"Cold out?" Paul asked, not turning his eyes from the screen.

Women have killed for less.

Snow Teen

There are moments, I believe, that not only require embracing our "inner child," but also beckoning the irresponsible and fearless teenager that lurks deeply beneath the stodgy, middle-age exteriors that encase many of us.

The kid who never wore a bicycle helmet, drove far too fast into the night without headlights "just to see if I could do it, Officer," and the kid I once was: tearing bareback through summer fields with girlfriends, collapsing into our horses' manes with laughter, certain that we would always be 14 and perpetually in love with Peter Frampton.

Two mornings after our recent snowfall, before sunrise, my rubber muck boots cracking through the frozen crust on the way to the barn, I made my way gingerly toward the routine of morning chores: feeding and cleaning stalls, breaking the ice in water buckets and re-adjusting blankets.

It is so rare to experience a moment of perfect stillness, I find. Even determined efforts of meditation and prayer are often interrupted by the shrill of the telephone or the wandering thought of checking e-mail or the flash of worry over a bill forgotten to be paid. However, this particular morning, my path illuminated by a full moon suspended confidently above the pink-tinged horizon, beckoned me out of the barn after throwing everyone their breakfast hay, to lean against the paddock gate and absorb the perfection of the undisturbed mantle of white over the gentle swell of hills of the larger pasture.

The 14-year-old, unseen yet keenly felt, dared me to retrieve the "Flexible Flier" leaning against the wall in the garden shed, and I answered her smirk with one of my own and, in a matter of moments, found myself sitting upon my old, wooden, friend, red steel runners poised and ready for the descent that is second only to the Saluda Grade and punctuated with massive oaks and poplars. The snow, frozen and hard, would offer no help at slowing us should I panic, and I chose to sit instead of lying flat, steering with my feet and holding the baling-twine rope between my work-gloved hands.

The posture of choice for most humans, when frightened, is a forward, cowering, collapse that becomes fetal, and I heard myself bark out loud as I would to a riding student:

"Sit up straight! Chest first!" and shoved myself forward with hands on either side of the sled.

In a flash I was over the crest and hurtling down the hill behind the barn at breathtaking speed. The stillness of the morning was pierced by a sharp intake of breath as I barely negotiated the path around the heavy limb of an oak and flying over an empty creek bed at the bottom of the hill, softer snow was flung upward, stinging my eyes. Mounting the hill on the other side, the sled slowed, came to a stop and began sliding backward. Gulping for air and dissolving into laughter, I followed its journey, letting go of the rope and lying down, sliding back down the incline and coming to a final halt in a few feet. The moon, now tangled in the branches of the poplar above me, seemed to grin in approval, and I remained flat on my back, grinning back and in no particular hurry to rise to my feet and begin the day in earnest. A "V" of geese flew overhead. In the barn, impatient hooves began to hammer against stall doors, anxious for grain and an explanation of why they were considered too fragile for such larking about in icy conditions.

"I'll see you sometime," I said to the 14-year-old, but she was gone. Pulling the "Flier" behind me as I trudged up the hill to the barn, I glanced once over my shoulder and thought I caught a glimpse of her but wasn't sure. It would be criminal to let too much time pass before calling her back again.

Corn Queen

Recently, I had lunch with a friend who brought along her friend who was introduced to me, along with a merry face full of mirth, as having once been crowned "Sparkle City Snow Queen."

I would open a vein to own that sash and crown. I'm not a beautiful woman. Never have been. Reality descended upon me, rather gently, in the reply my mother once gave me in a department store when, looking dejectedly over training bras that were too large, I asked simply, "Am I beautiful?"

The nanosecond of hesitation my mother gave was all that was needed to seal my fate. Being an artist, my mother answered with what she considered to be a far more important attribute:

"You have character."

Well, just shoot me in the head.

I knew exactly what character meant. Carol, the receptionist from the old "Bob Newhart Show," had character. Pippy Longstocking had character. For heaven's sake, Ichabod Crane had character.

When you're 12 years old and going through an appalling puberty with which only Chelsea Clinton can empathize, you want to be told you're as lovely as Marcia Brady. You want to be the ethereal Kate Bush. You want to be beautiful. You want, oh, Lord, you want, just once in your life, during a great hair day, to be Sparkle City Snow Queen.

My manager, by whom I've been represented since 1988, entered several pageants to pay her way through college and, eventually, earn a master's in music. She has always threatened to kill me if I give away her secret shame, but in not publishing her name, I think it's quite all right to tell you she was once crowned Miss Corn Queen.
Not only did she receive the tiara and sash and several hundred dollars, she was given the use of a brand-new Chrysler K car for a whole year ... with "Carolina Corn Queen" emblazoned on the sides.

"I was horrified," she confessed.

"I would be too," I agreed, nodding sympathetically. "I would have worn a bag over my head rather to have been seen driving a K car."

"Not the car," she snapped. "The stupid 'Corn Queen' banner on its sides."

Oh. See, I would have been gloriously proud of being named Carolina Corn Queen. I would let the title define me for the rest of my natural life. If I were being bumped off a flight, I would draw myself up to full height and say haughtily to the airline reservationist, "Clearly you don't realize I'm the Corn Queen."

Jockeying for a spot in a crowded mall parking lot, I'd gesture to the side of my car and bark, "Corn Queen coming through!" If I were having a terrible day, what better therapy than to blow the dust off one's crown and sash and parade up and down the hall, hand on hip, still in my ratty bath robe, reliving those halcyon memories?

And as demeaning as many women feel pageants are, I suspect quite a few would secretly be delighted in being documented as the most beautiful woman amongst a group of candidates.

Why? Because these are the women who get ahead just a touch easier in life. Blessed with the same smarts and sense of humor, really attractive women seem to have the stars aligned on their side.

But that's OK. No one ever said life was fair. There's plenty of us gals out there with character that are doing just fine.

But you can't tell me Janet Reno wouldn't have killed to be Corn Queen.

A Novel Idea

If there's one thing I'm known for it is my penchant for trawling thrift stores and church sales for an interesting book.

Don't be fooled into thinking I'm what you might call "well read" — while I have dutifully absorbed Dickens and Hardy and Trollope there are millions of other books I've yet to touch. Perhaps it is this gaping yawn of knowledge I lack that inclines me to pick up such unlikely publications as "British Escort Ships of WWII" or "Ferns of the Coastal Carolinas," but really, to be honest, there's also a great dollop of nosiness involved as well.

You see, very often when you pick up a particularly old book something stuck between the pages, eons ago, falls into your lap just as you are settling upon the sofa to enjoy your read.

Opening a book of poetry, I once found page after page filled with pressed wildflowers. My mind began to dream with far more ambition than the poems themselves actually inspired — who put these flowers there? Was it a young girl, given the book by an admirer that, upon a summer walk, was presented with a token bouquet and, overwhelmed by her sweetheart's offering, decided to keep them forever? Were the poems upon where the flowers rested of great significance? Or was she a lonely spinster who lived a life of dashed romantic hopes?

Beginning an early La Carre' mystery, I found nestled between the front pages a stiff, black-bordered card with the name of a priest printed at the bottom beginning with the formidable 'Reverend.' In what could only be assumed to be his handwriting was this admonishing note to a parishioner:

"Next time you feel like picking up a bottle, pick up a good book instead."

Oh, my.

And recently, not of great importance but of simple amusement, I found within a copy of Noel Coward's "Present Indicative," a small envelope adorned with a 5-cent stamp and postmarked May 12, 1967 (the same date of which it was found!), in which housed a thank you note from a child to her Aunt which read:

"Thank you ever so much for the dollar you sent me Grandmom sent me 3 dollars I spent 2 so now I have three again because Aunt Nancy sent me one. Please come and visit us soon. We go to school 15 more days.
Your Neice,
Penny"

Clearly "Grandmom" had trumped all others with her generosity, but what struck me was the pleasure a single dollar could bring to a child in 1967. No worries of which video games to buy or computer upgrades. Just a single greenback. I was probably Penny's age in 1967 and one felt terribly wealthy with a dollar tucked into one's patent leather red coin purse. It could buy an awful lot!

And even today, in a thrift shop, it can usually buy one heck of an adventure.

The Christmas Nest

Sometimes God gives you a little present.

Well, actually, I believe He gives us gifts all the time; it's just that we seldom recognize them. Furthermore, it is astonishing how the smallest thing can stir the heart and quell the stress and the grievances of our daily lives.

Like many of you, I too have had a challenging year: accidents that necessitated trips to the ER, sick animals, broken water pipes, exploding septic tanks, a missing cat (I still believe she is alive) and putting down a cherished horse of 29 years, Moose. Most of these calamities demanded hefty payments and, naturally, finances are tighter than normal, and it was with a rather bleak heart that I contemplated Christmas as I walked through the front field to bring the horses in for the evening.

It will be a pared-down holiday this year. Our annual tradition of gathering in a particularly lovely inn has been vetoed, and it was agreed by all to share in only the most modest of gift giving. Worst of all, donations to favorite charities will have to be smaller.

I've never been an extravagant gift buyer for Christmas, as it is my personal battle against commercialism. It's tremendously important to me, particularly as I grow older, to focus on the season of advent with careful introspection. However, to be honest, there is a dollop of paganism within me. I never feel I'm truly living unless smack-dab in the middle of nature, so I find great comfort in bringing armfuls of holly, pine and cedar into the house to decorate. It was these thoughts of finding a few more berries and pine cones to arrange along the mantle that made me sweep my eyes along the grass as I approached my horses, comfortably grazing, manes and tails filigreed in the late afternoon light.

It would have been so easy to miss, this tiny gift. But there, coiled tightly beside a tuft of dormant Bermuda, was the dearest little bird's nest, woven carefully with twigs and dried grass. And threaded within it was the unmistakable, coarse, white, tail hair of my old horse, Moose.

Placing it in the palm of my hand I was mesmerized by both its simplicity and beauty. It is such a little thing, fragile and charming, yet powerfully illustrating the circle of life.

May you, too, have a merry, little, Christmas.

About The Author

Syndicated columnist, Pam Stone, shares a selection of readers' favorites from her own "I'm Just Saying" in this charming collection which chronicles years of adventures on her 'Funny Farm' in the upstate of South Carolina.

Weary of the hustle and bustle of life in Los Angeles, the former co-star of the ABC series, 'Coach', comedian, and radio personality selected instead to live what she naively thought might be 'the quiet life' in a town of 2,000 residents. What followed are the honest to goodness (well, almost) accounts of this Upstate South Carolina experience.

Acknowledgements

Cover design by Christine Moore, Susan Tomkin

Cover photos by Tim Kimzey, Paul McAllister, Lester McNeely

"I'm Just Saying" by Pam Stone can currently be read in:

The Spartanburg Herald-Journal
The Tryon Bulletin
The Hendersonville Times
The Greenwood Index-Journal
The Myrtle Beach Sun
The Greer Citizen
The Gaston Gazette
The Shelby Star

Made in the USA
Charleston, SC
20 June 2012